OUTSIDE THE BOX

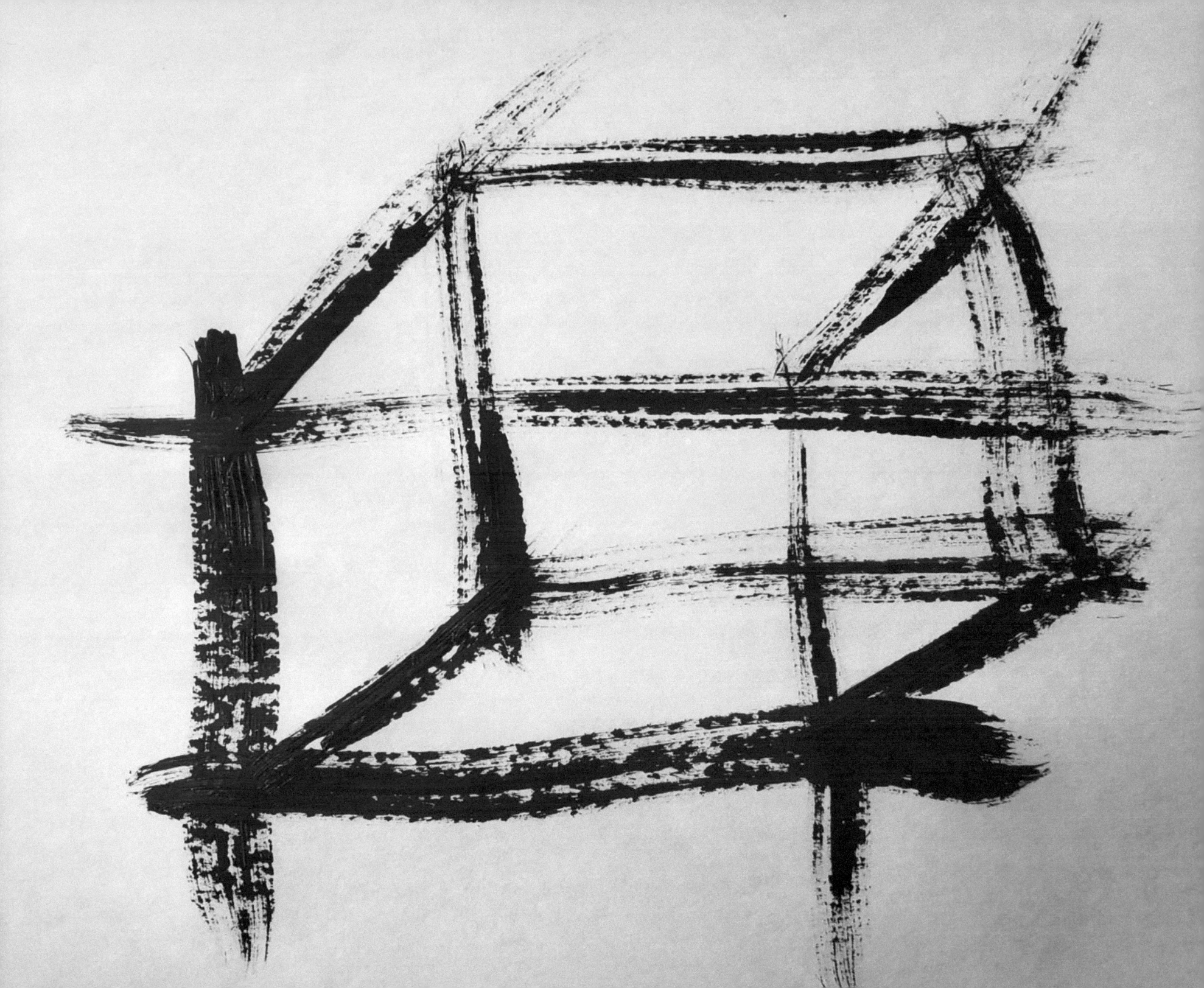

OUTSIDE THE BOX

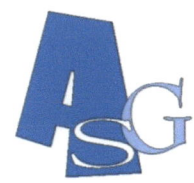

Publishing for Authors by Authors!

Vision

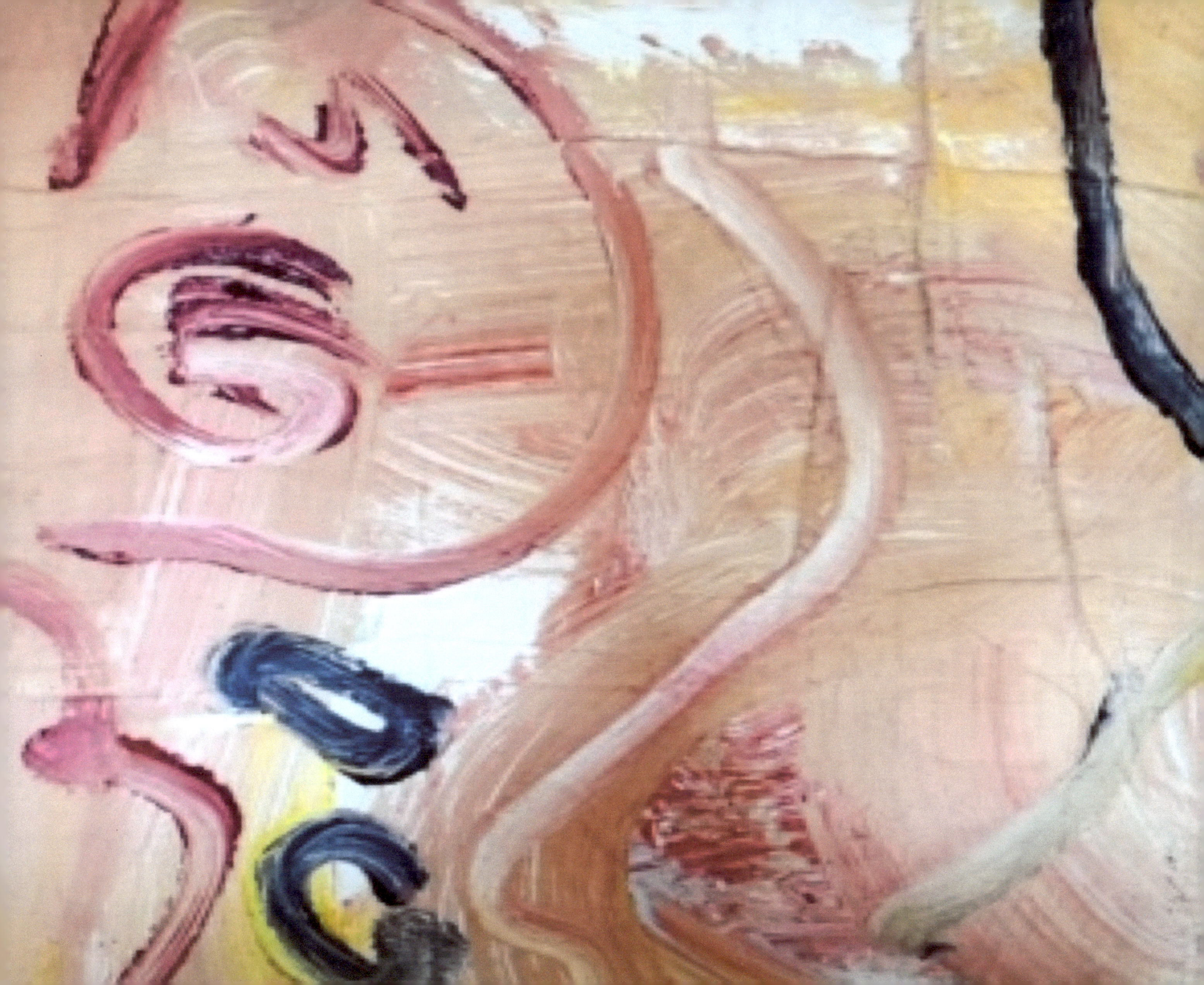

$$1 + 1 = 11$$

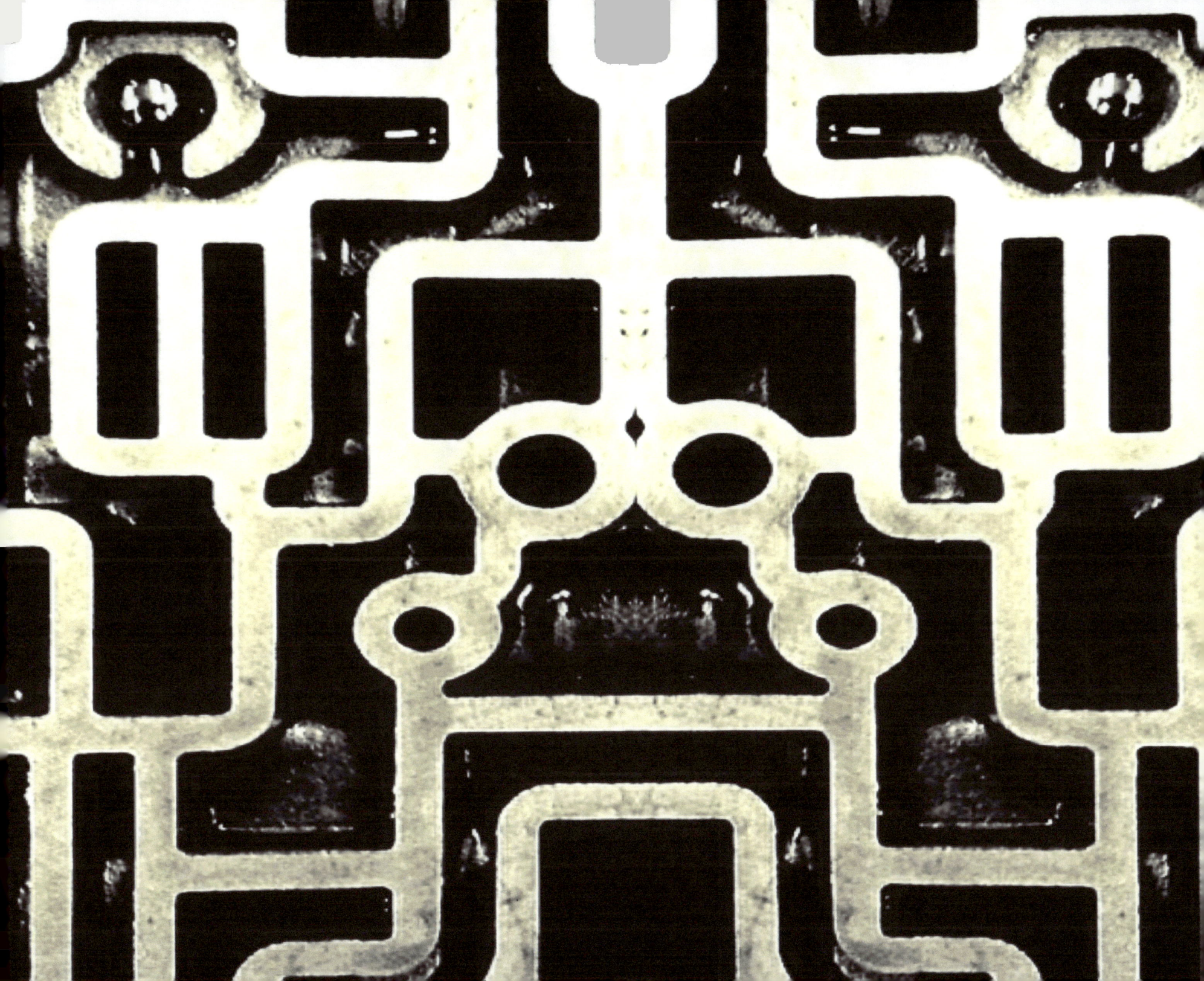

Psalms 82.6

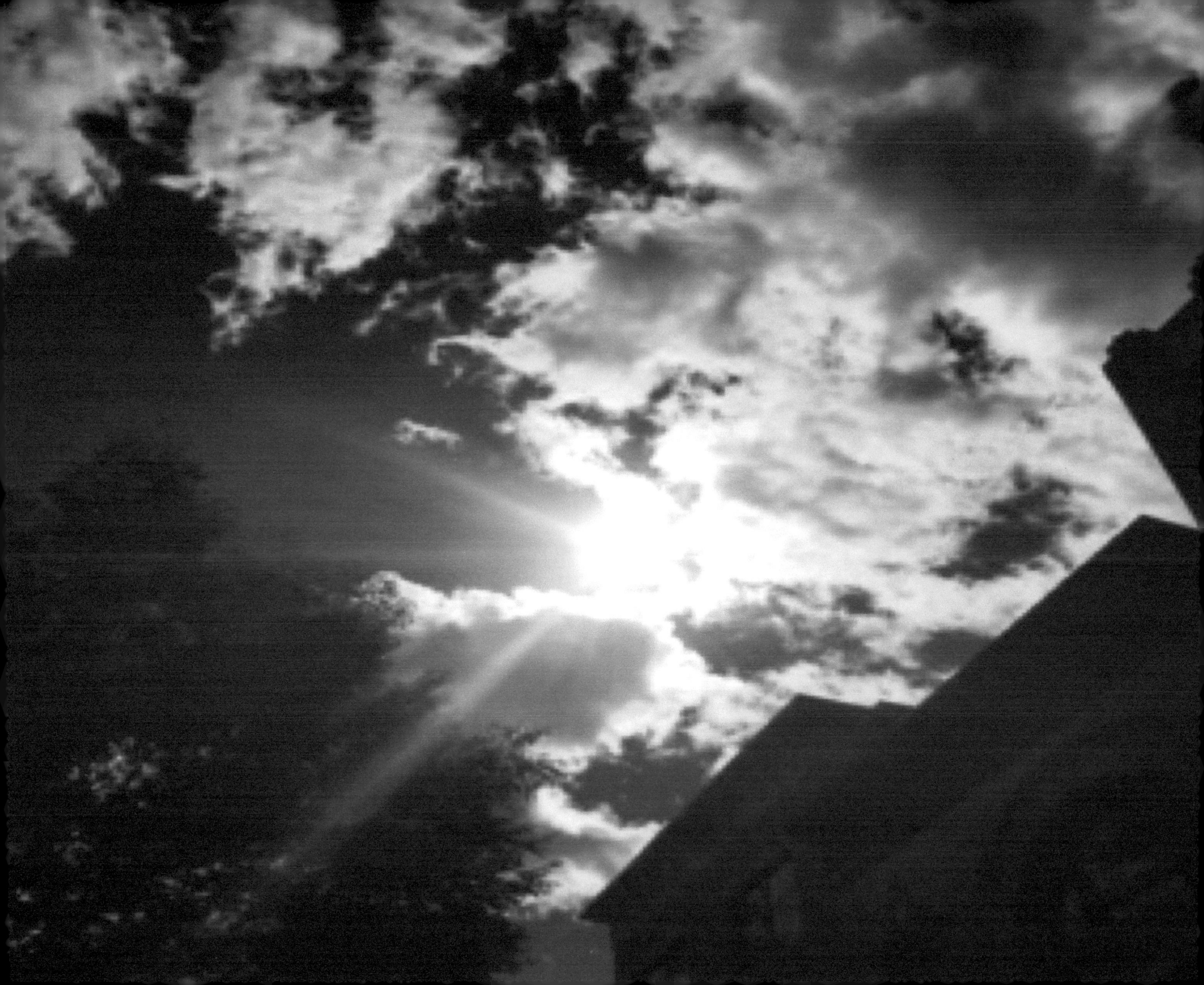

it's not a
one world..

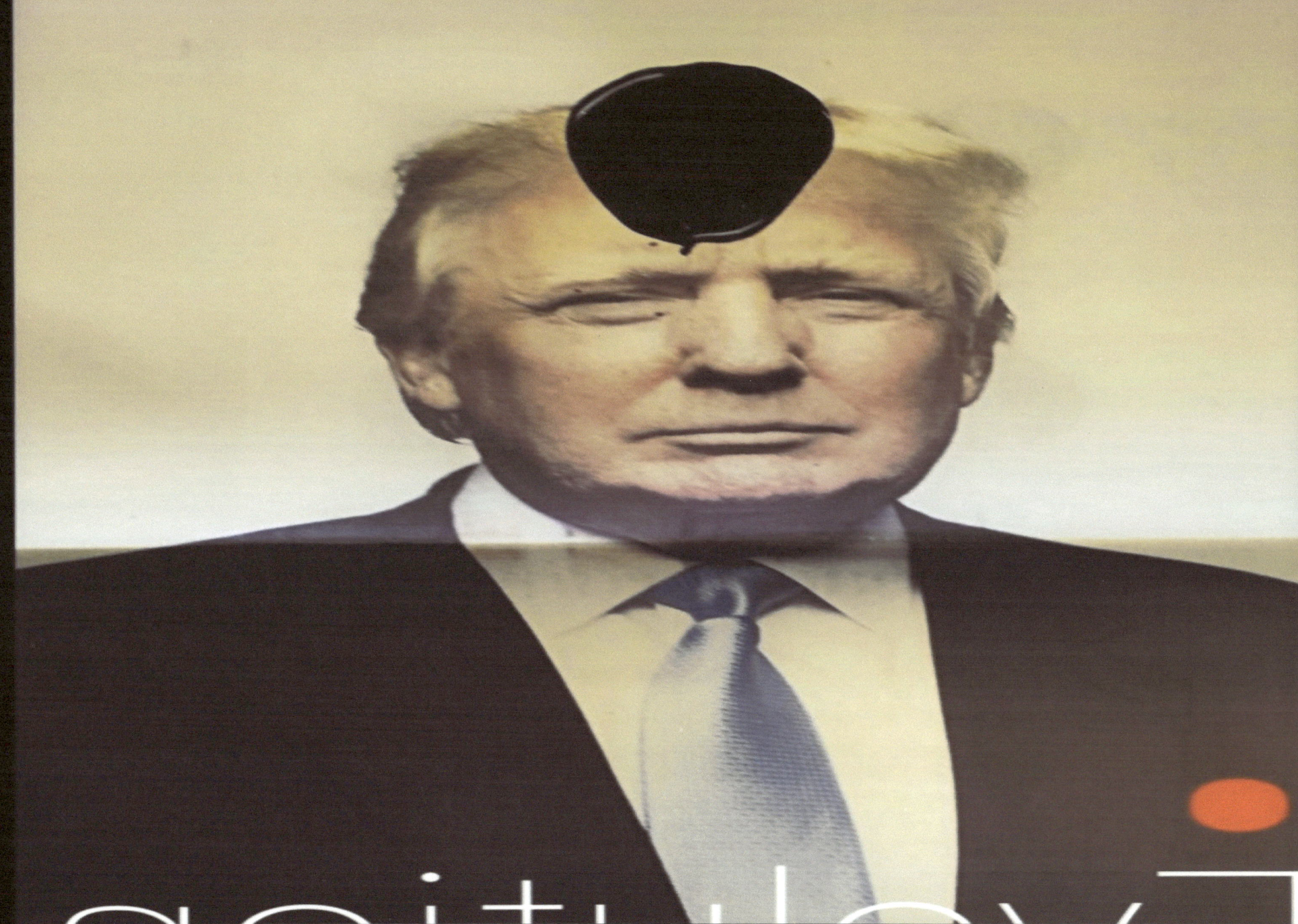

Warrior Living

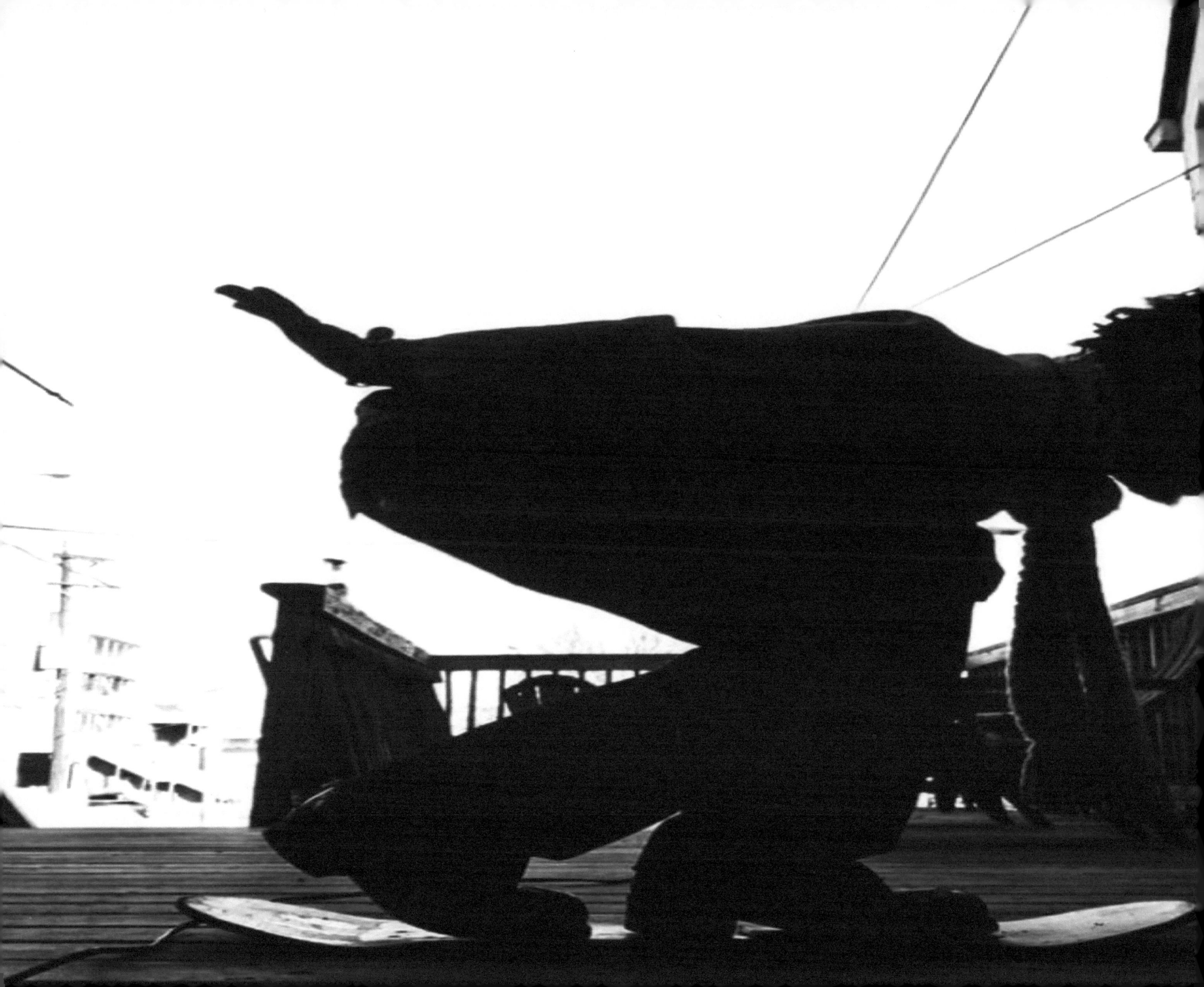

Women come and go,
But a Dragon stays for
Life.

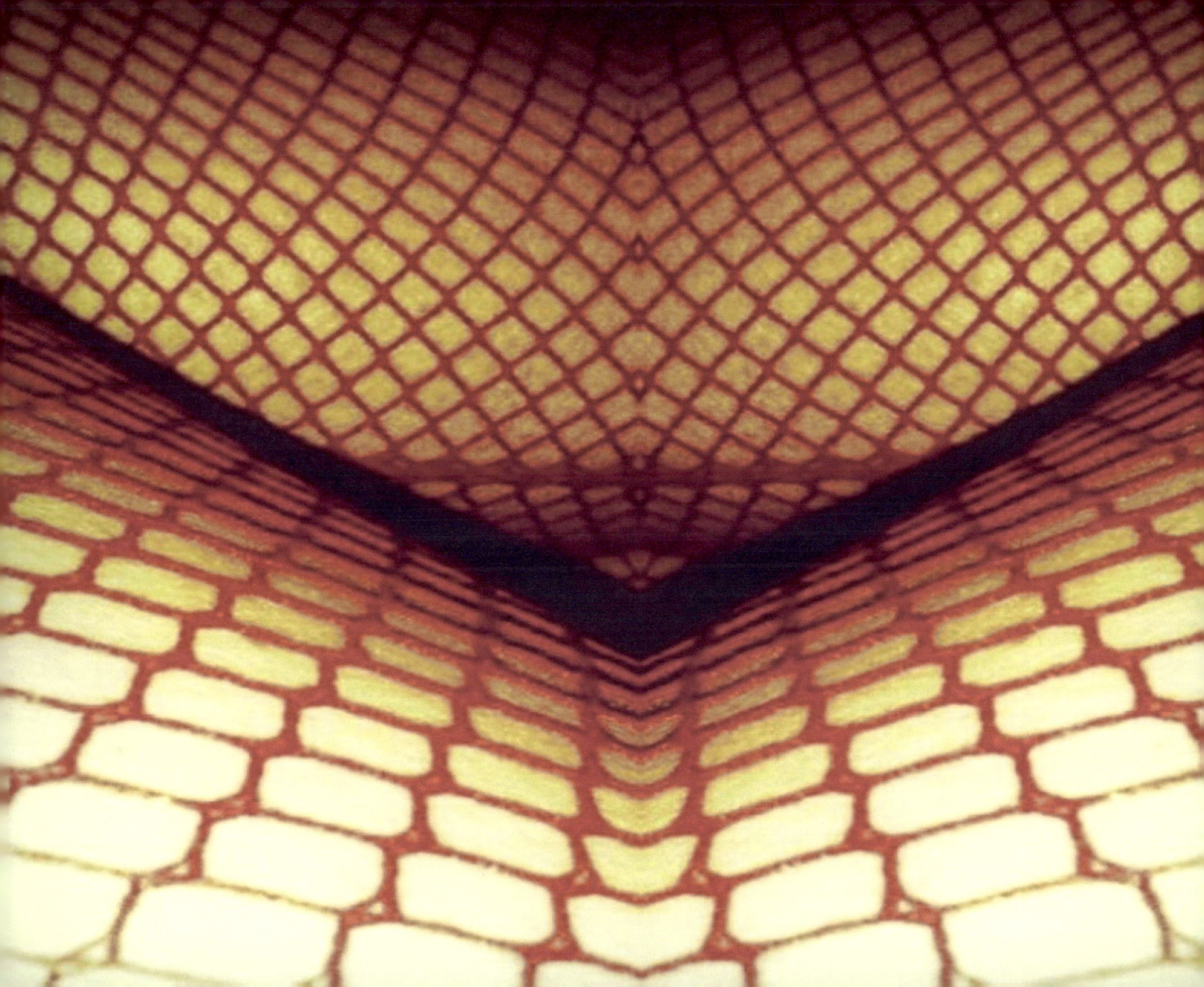

Trappd

(Thanks)

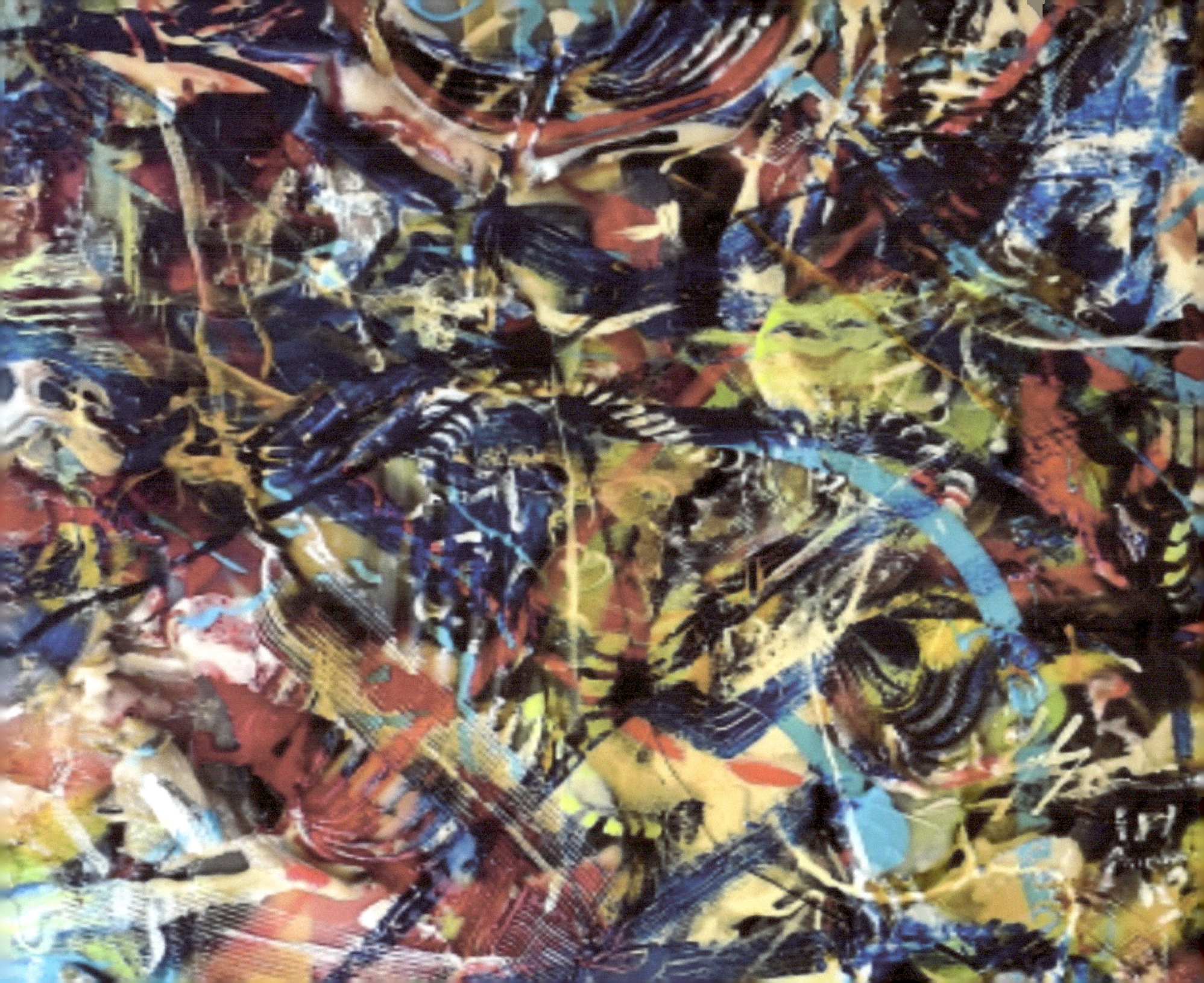

vote

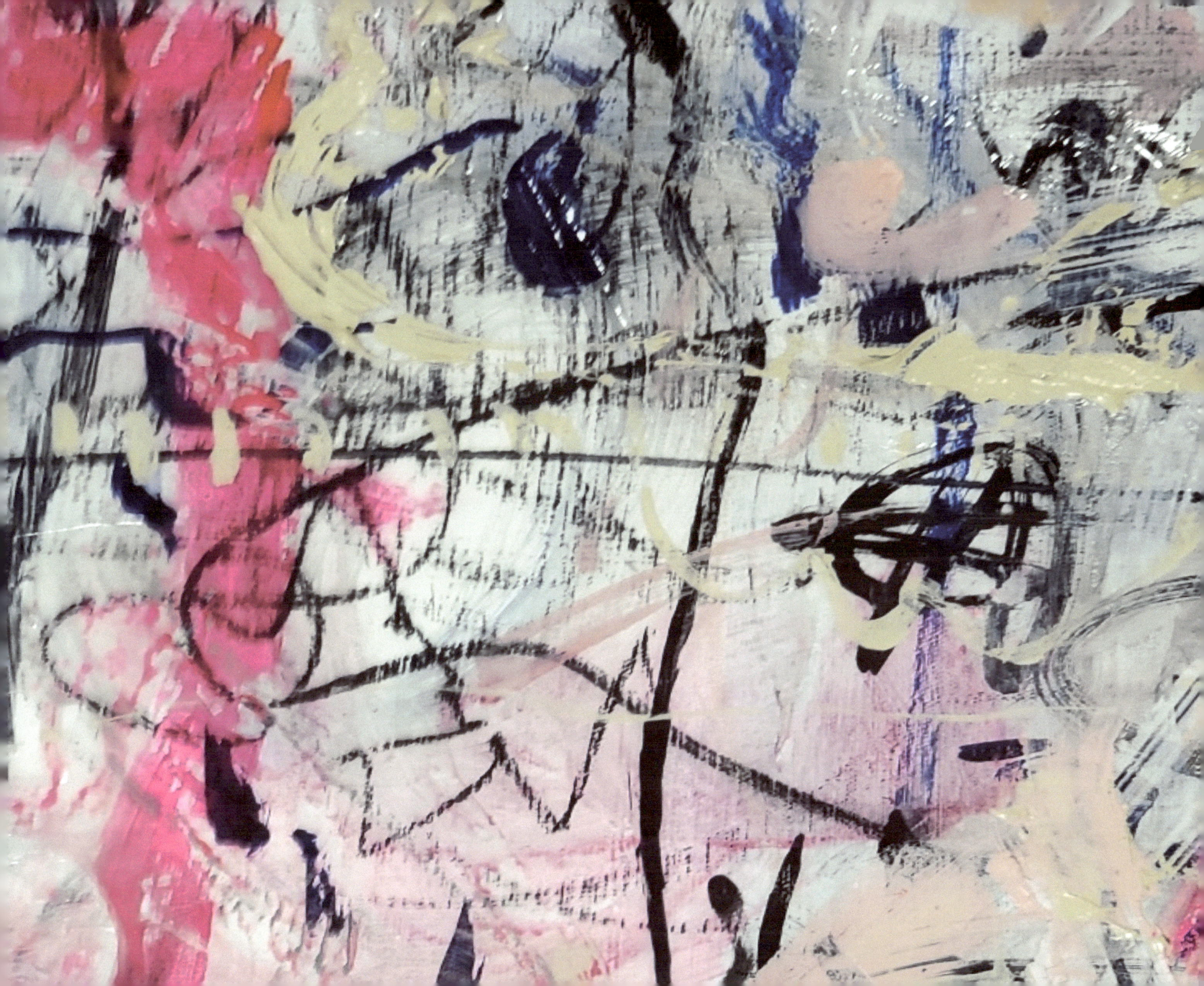

711

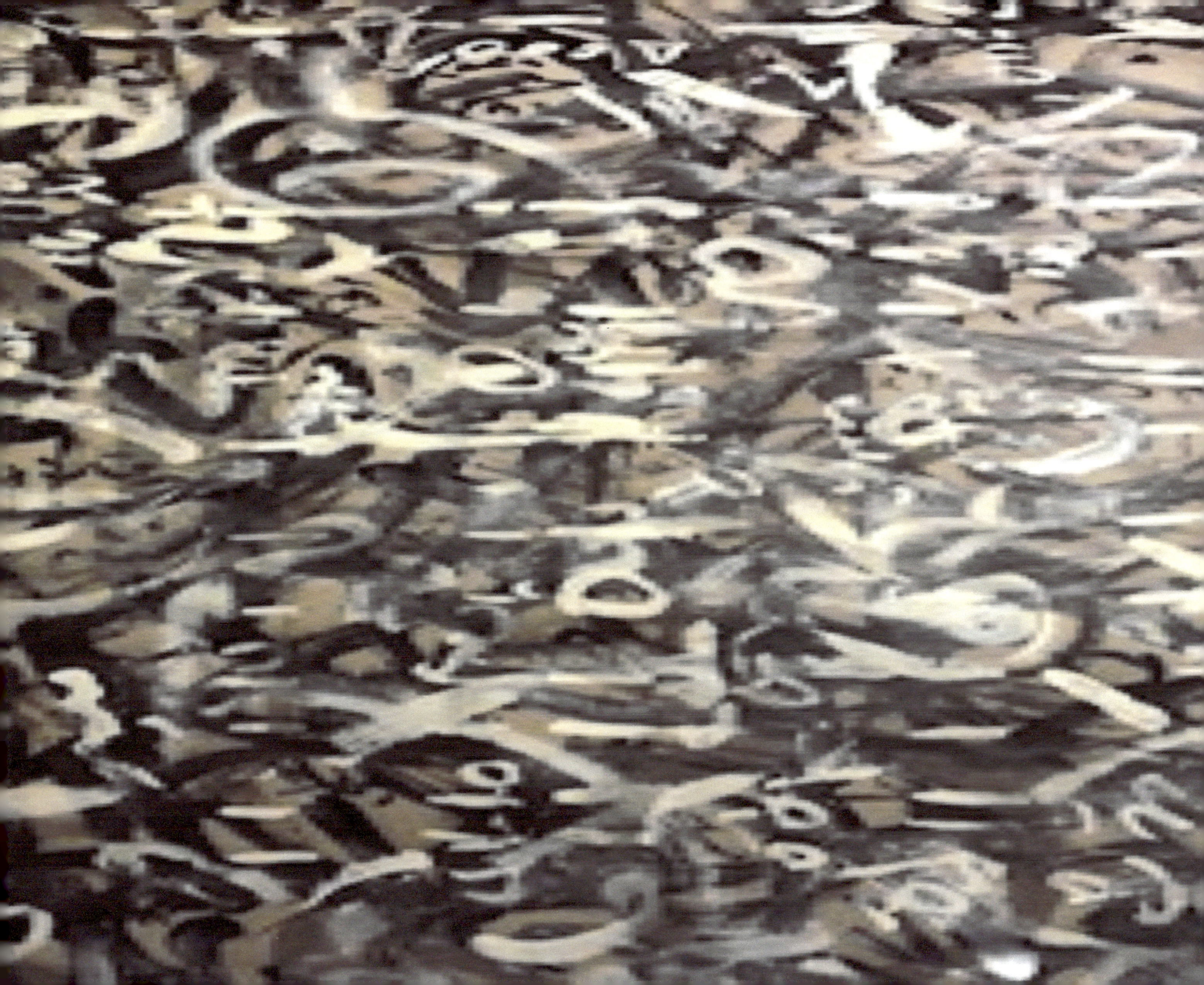

Single
Life

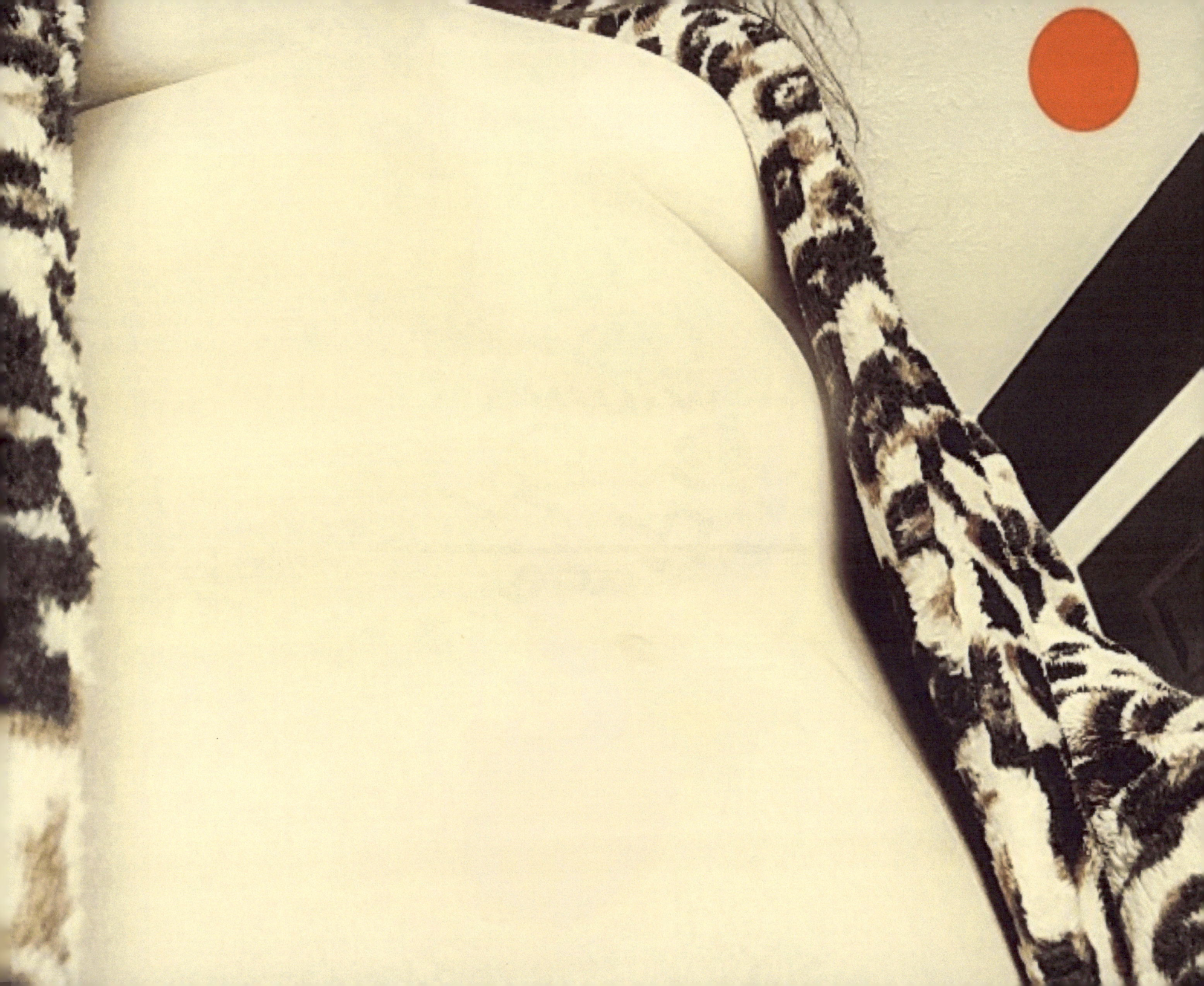

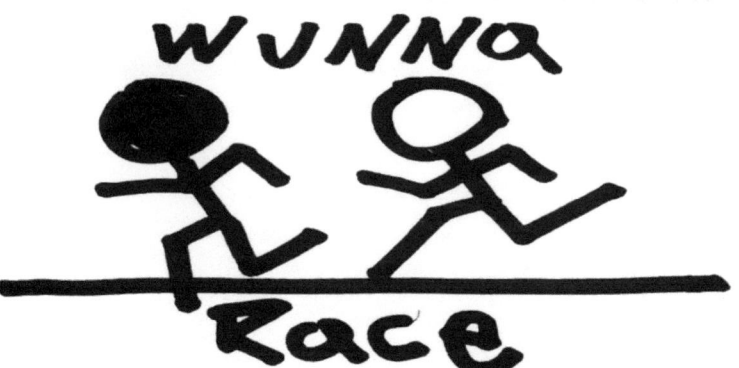

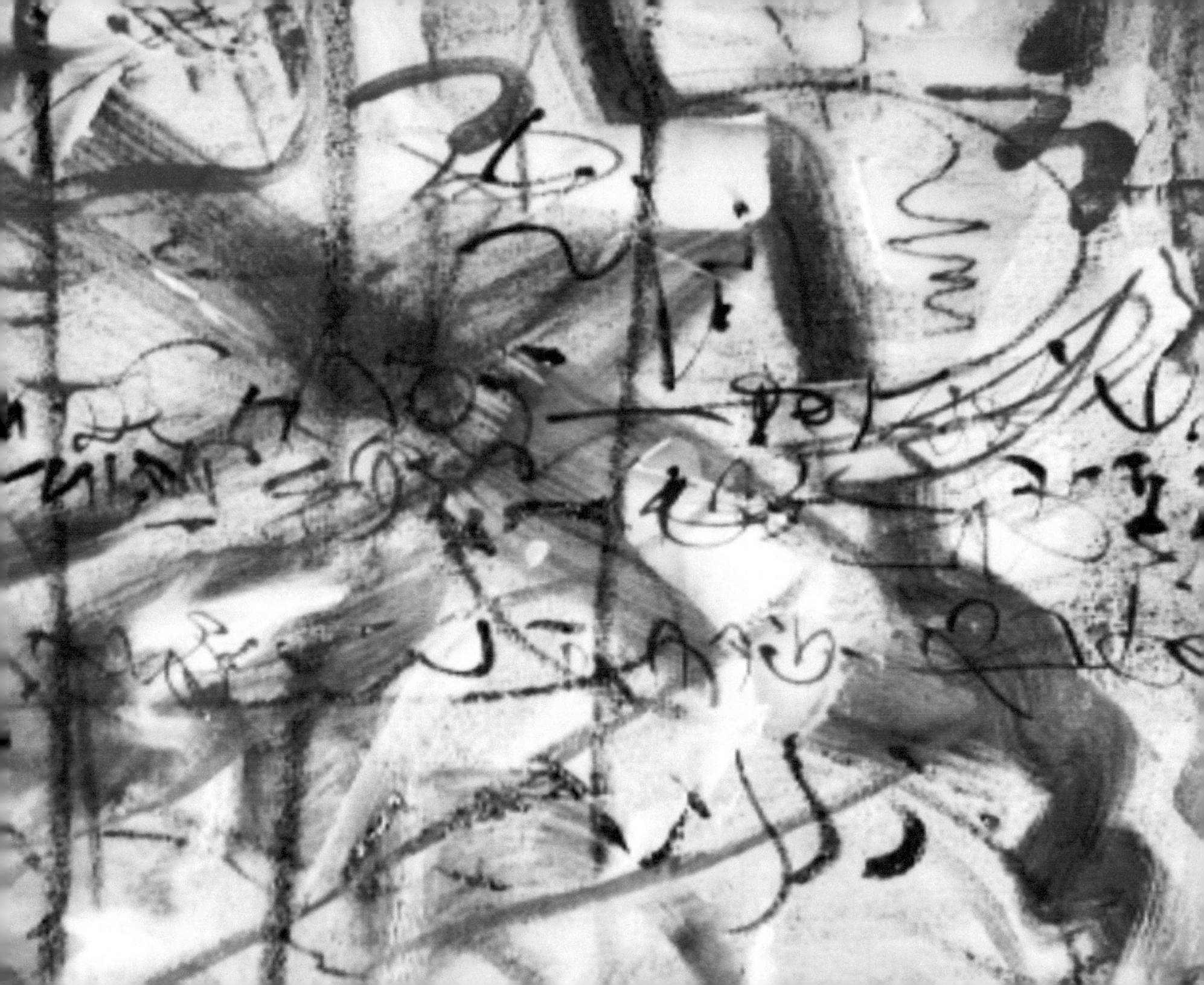

Fear
runs
Deep

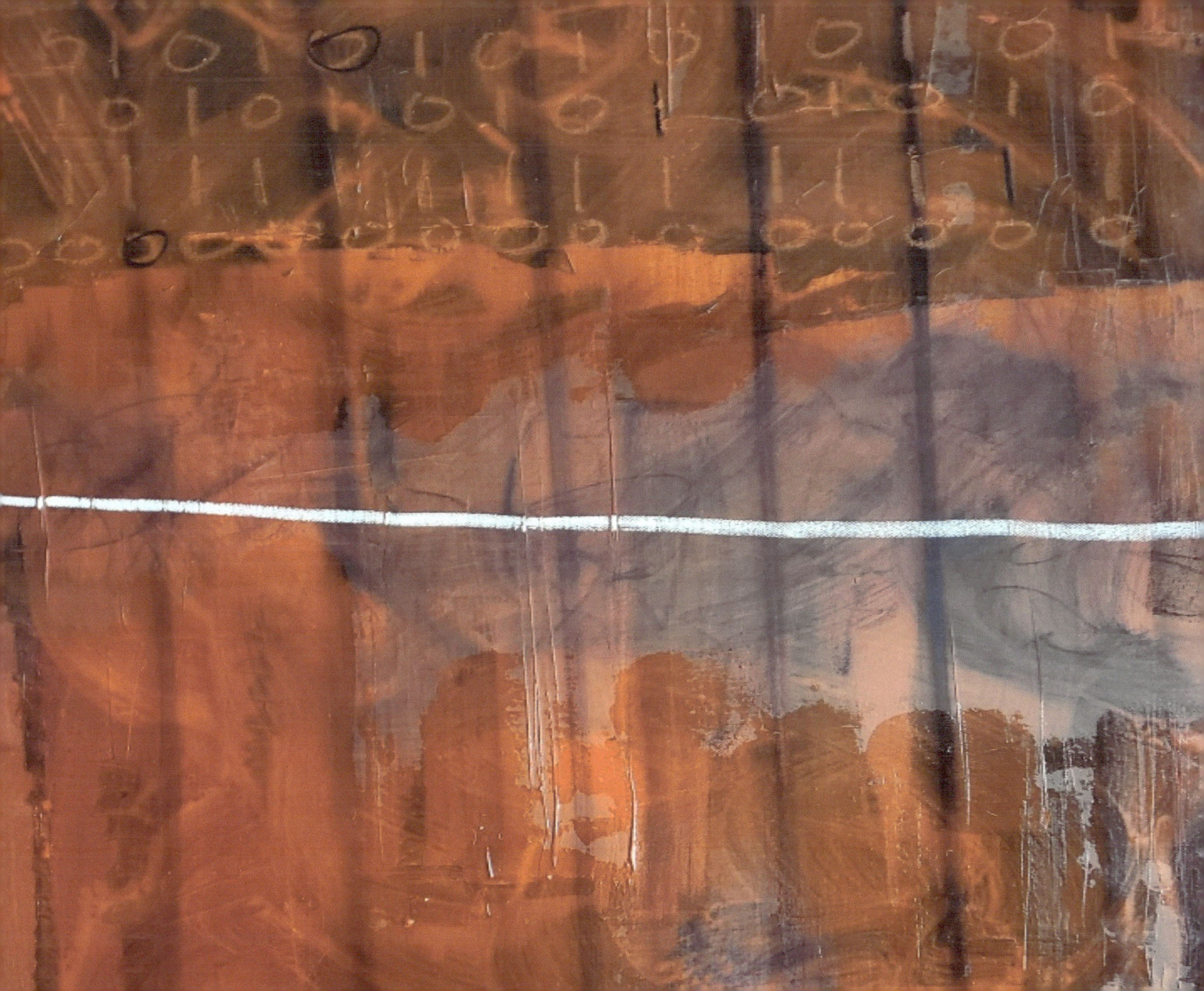

sex

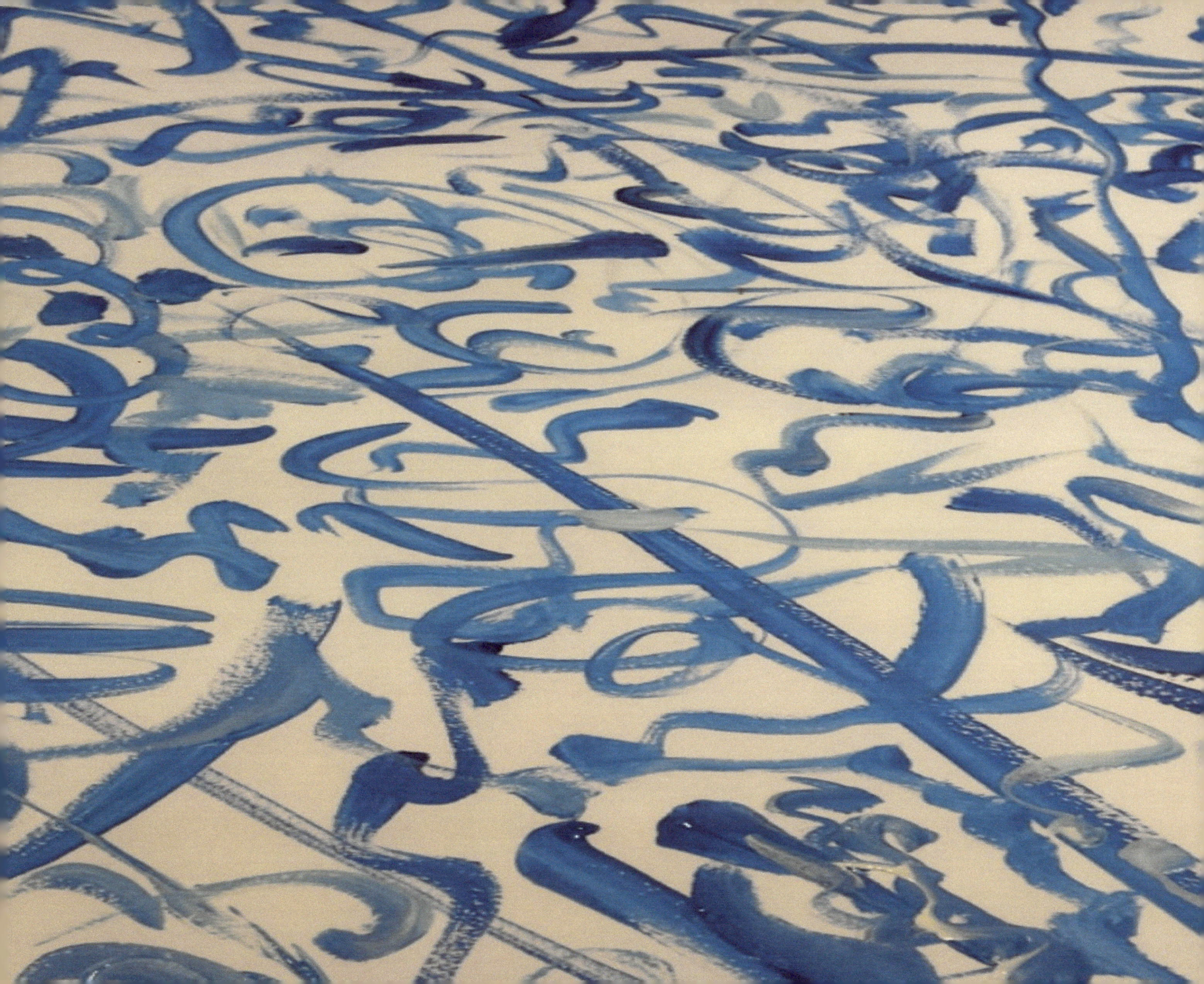

Right
ON!

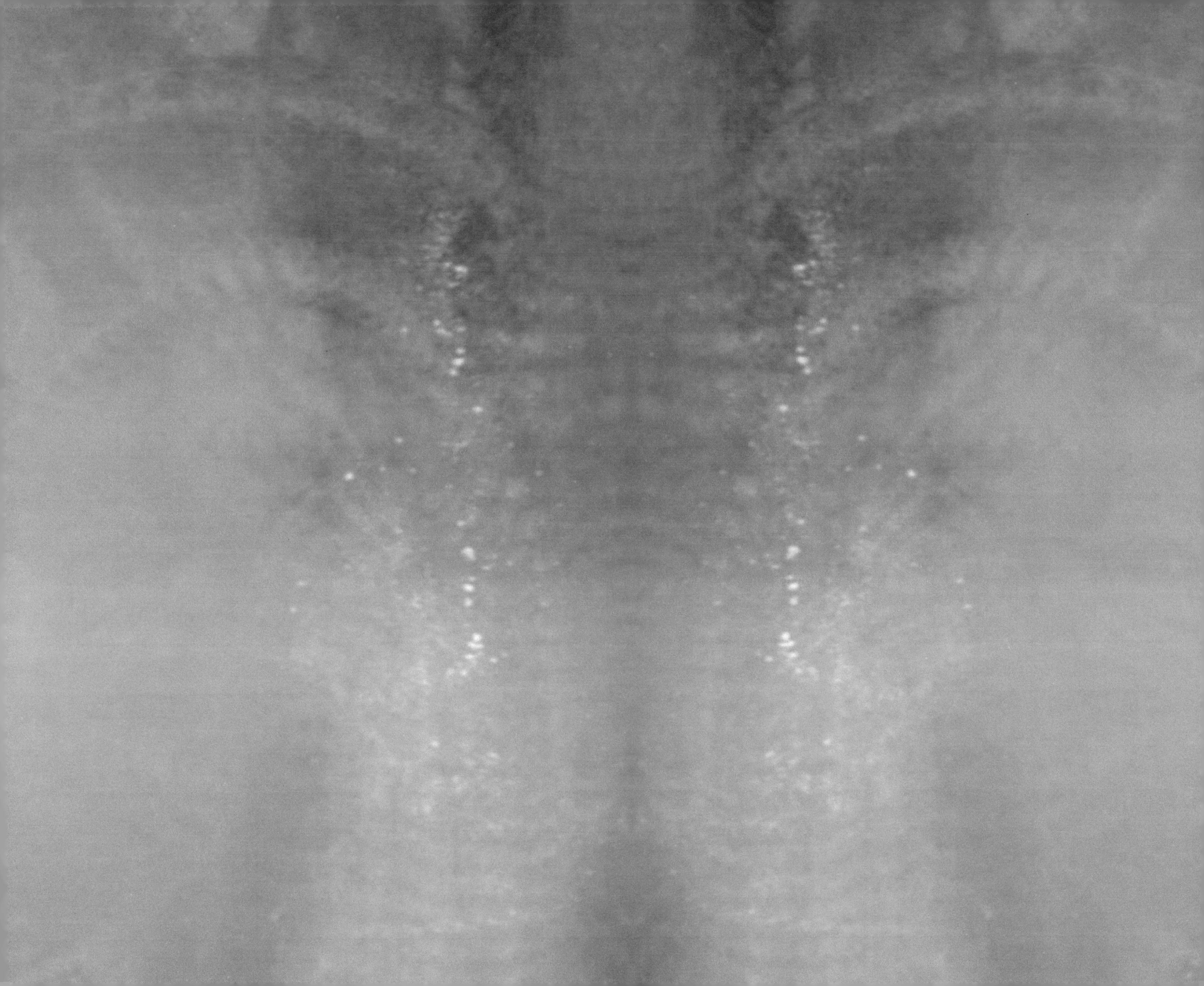

what is My
favorite Colour!
?

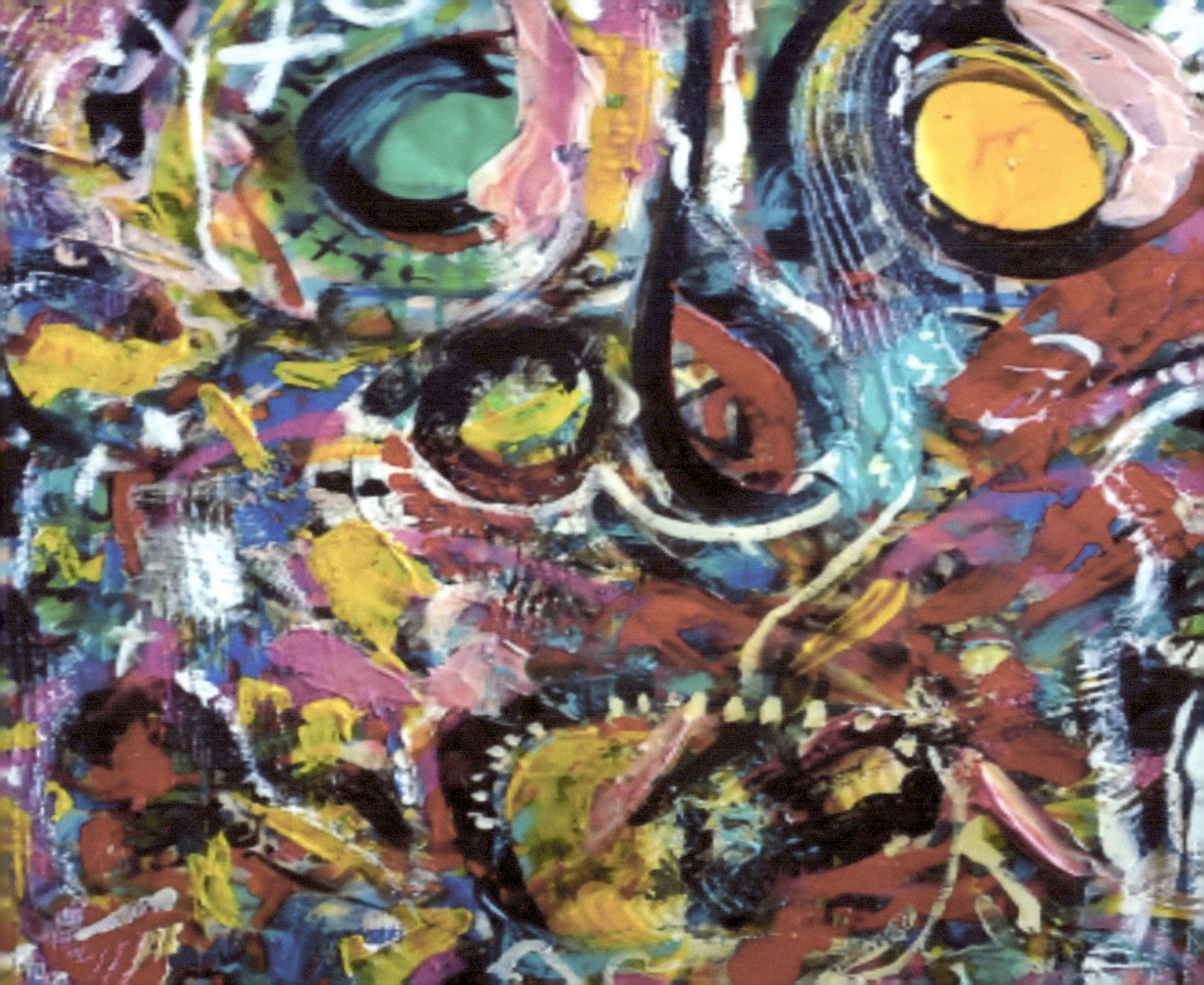

Pnuk it!

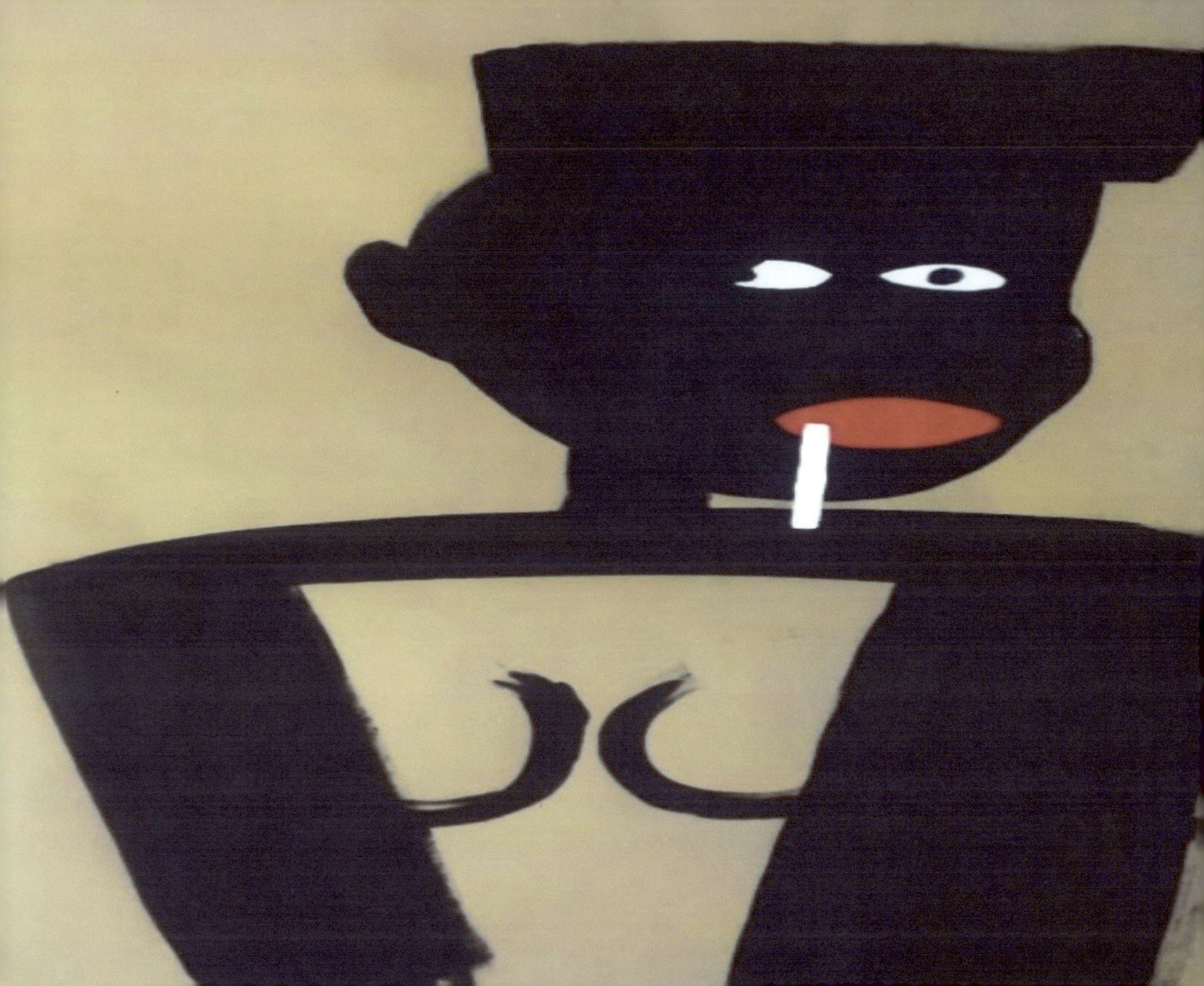

4360 Fist

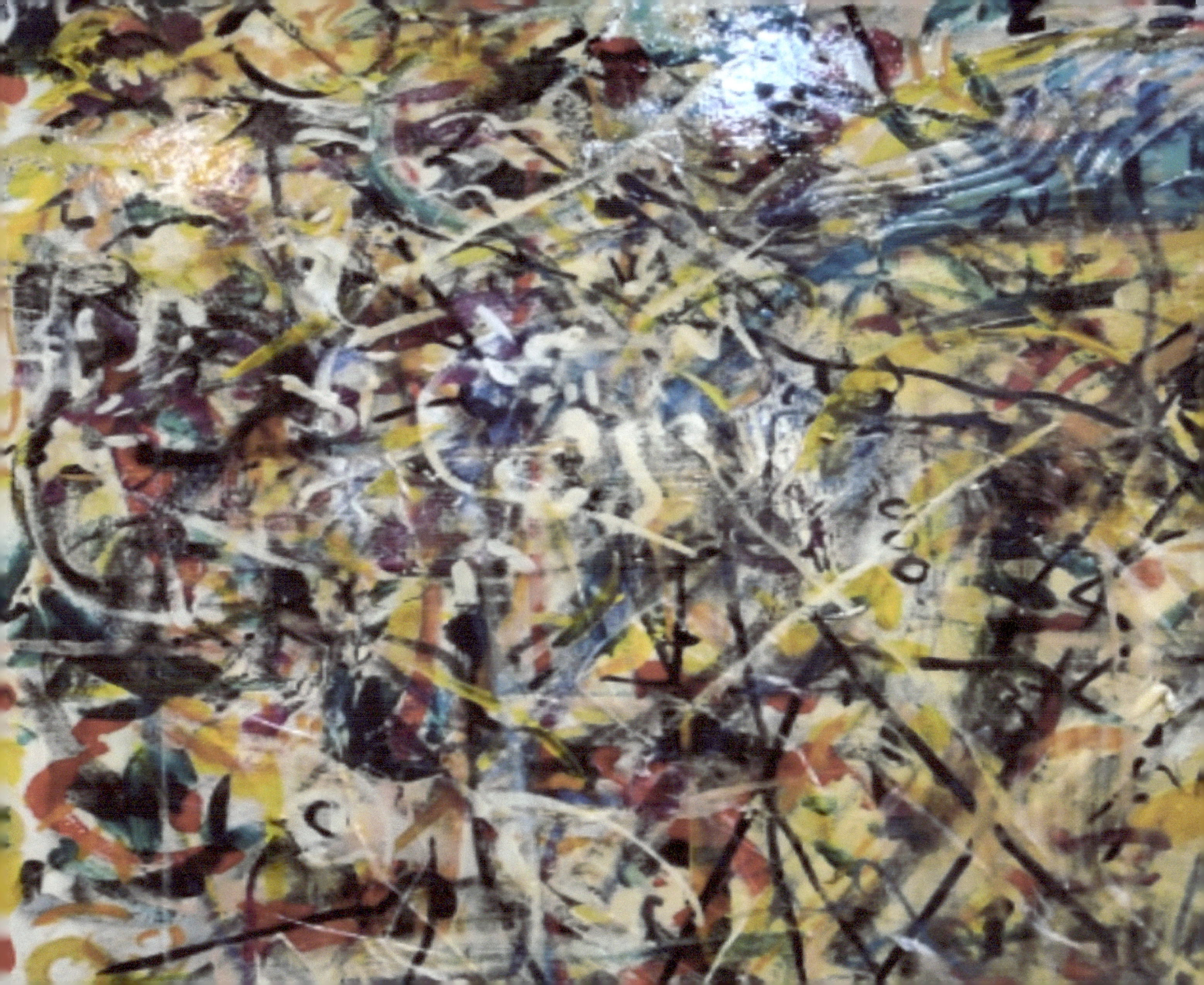

evolution

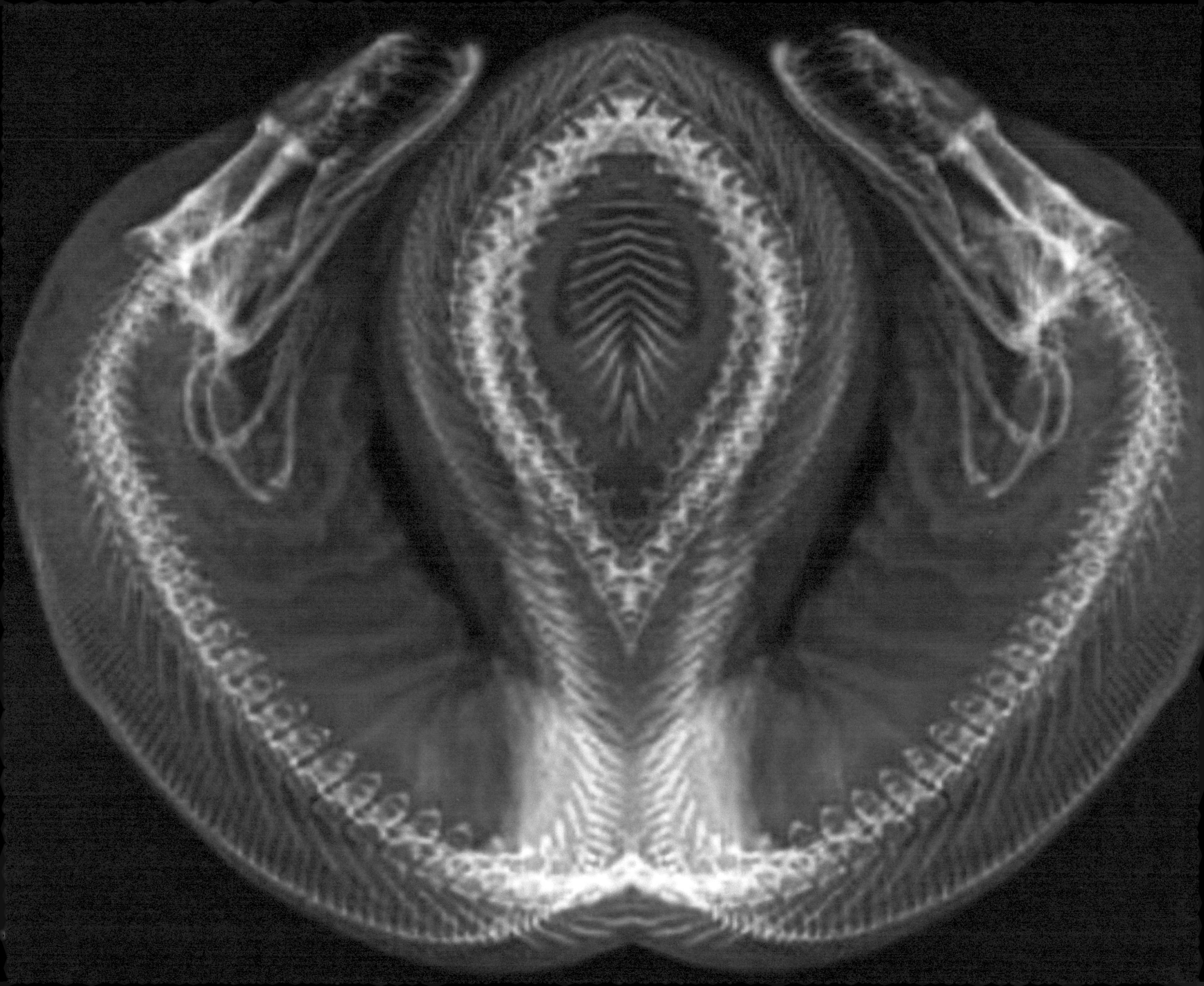

Gage

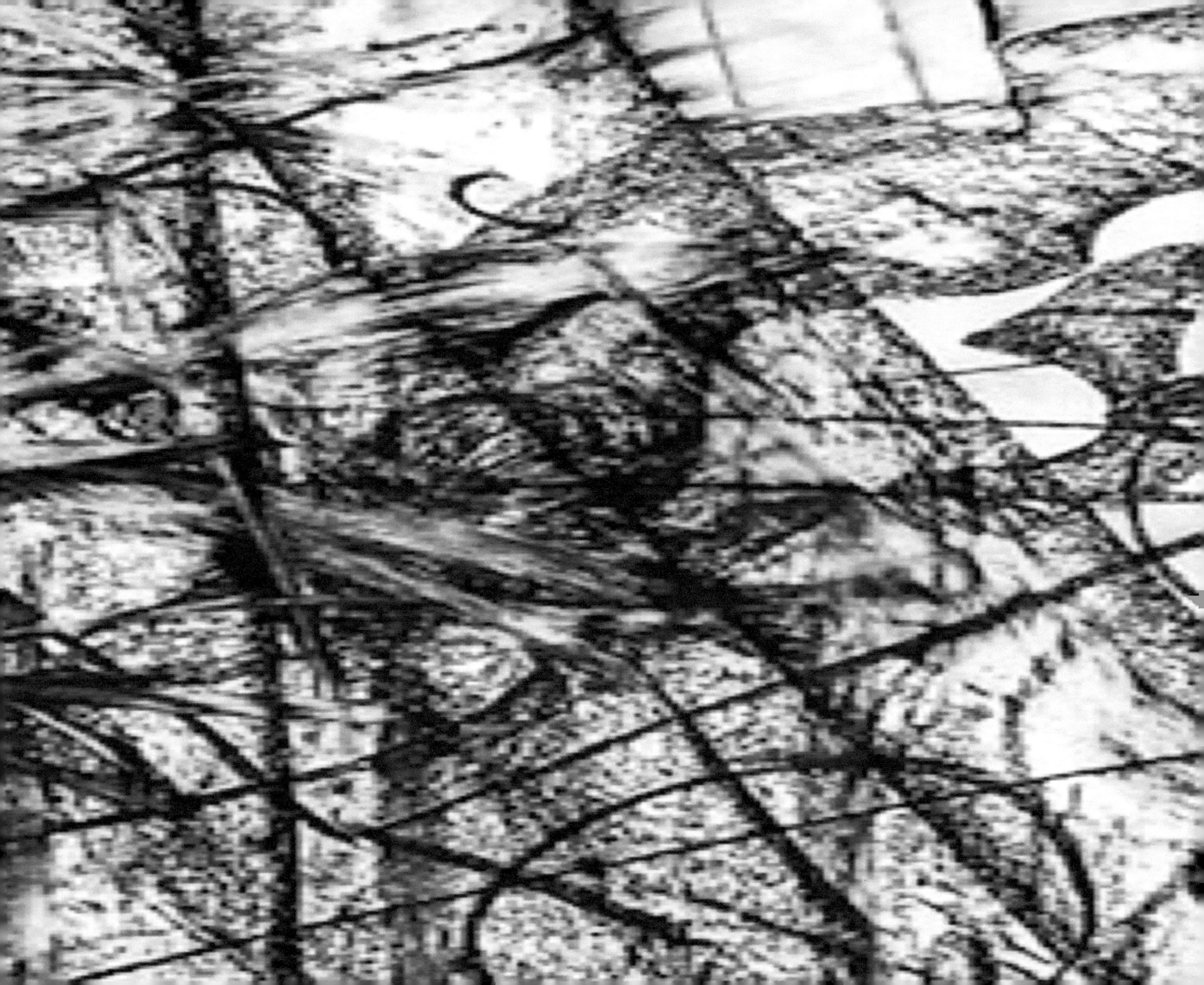

Love

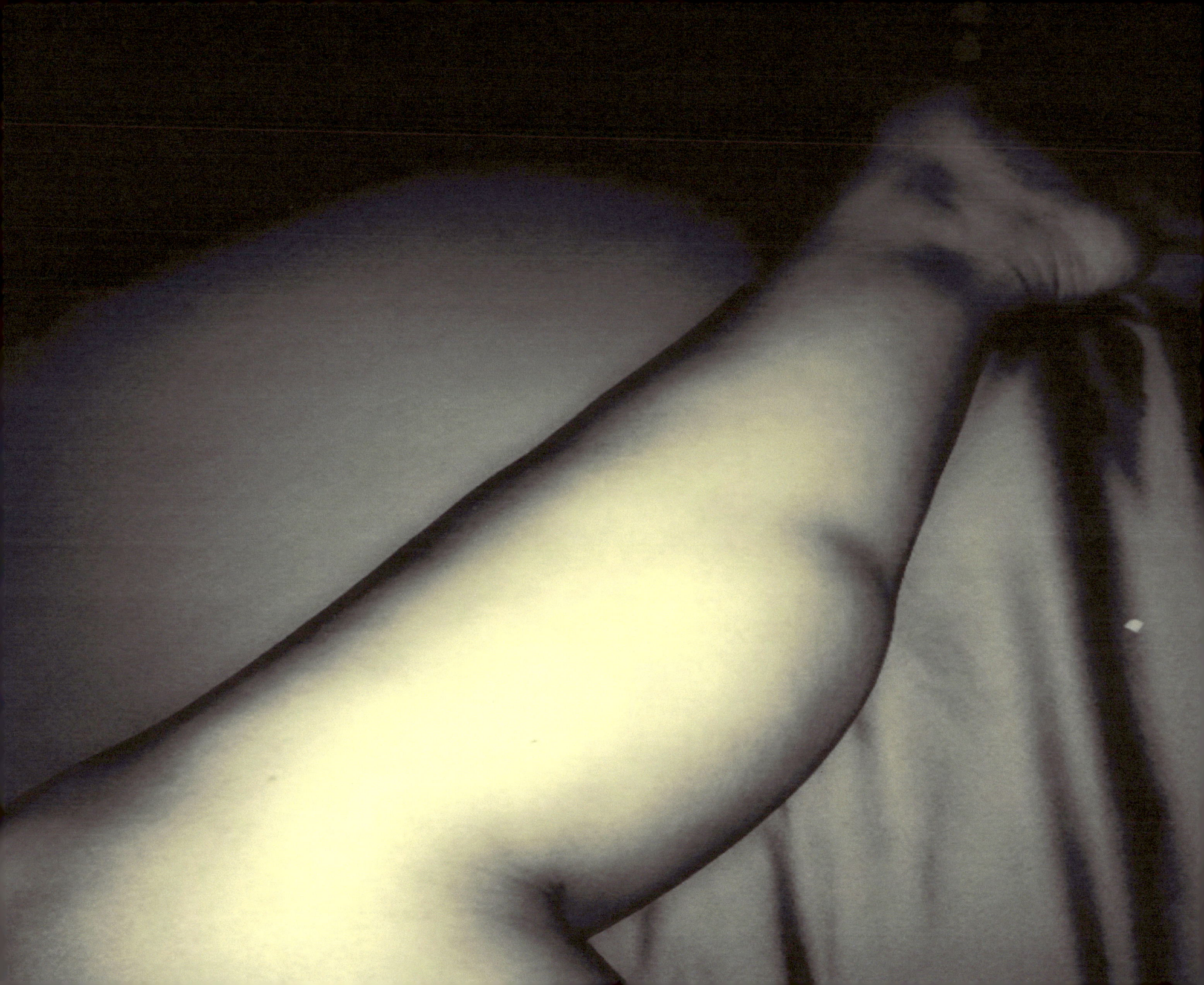

i Miss U
Mom.

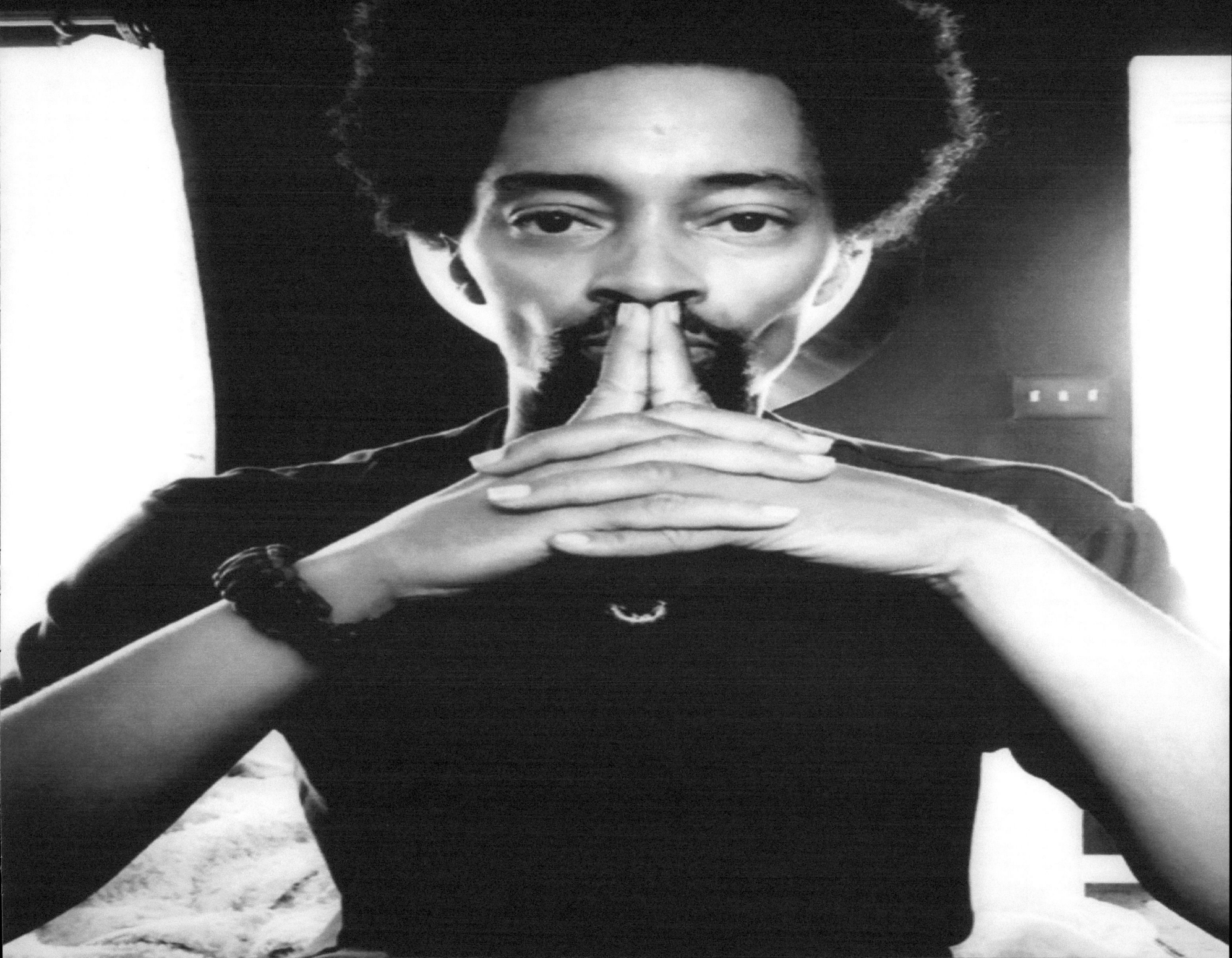

One more
thing!!!

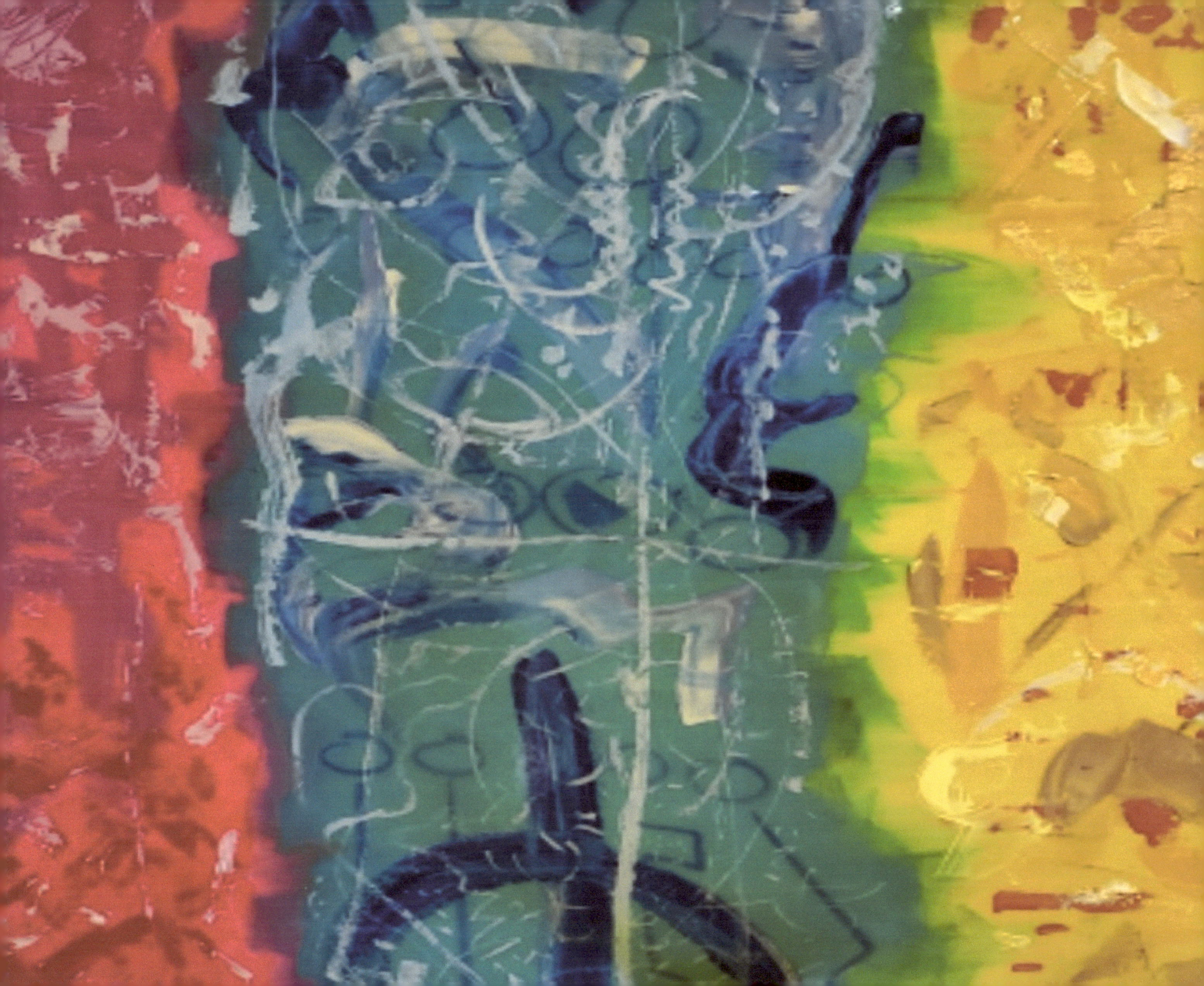

~~POWER~~

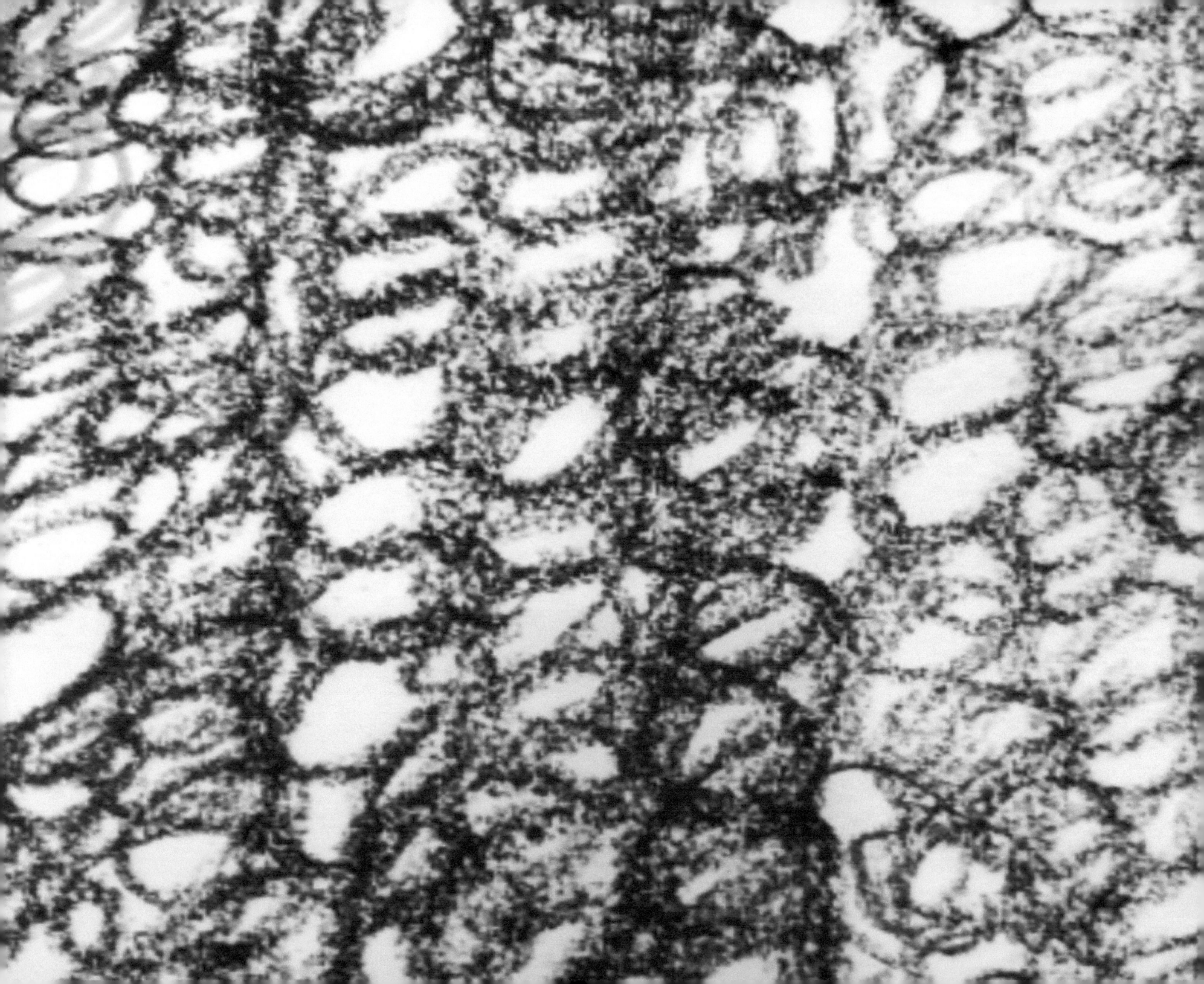

Fin.

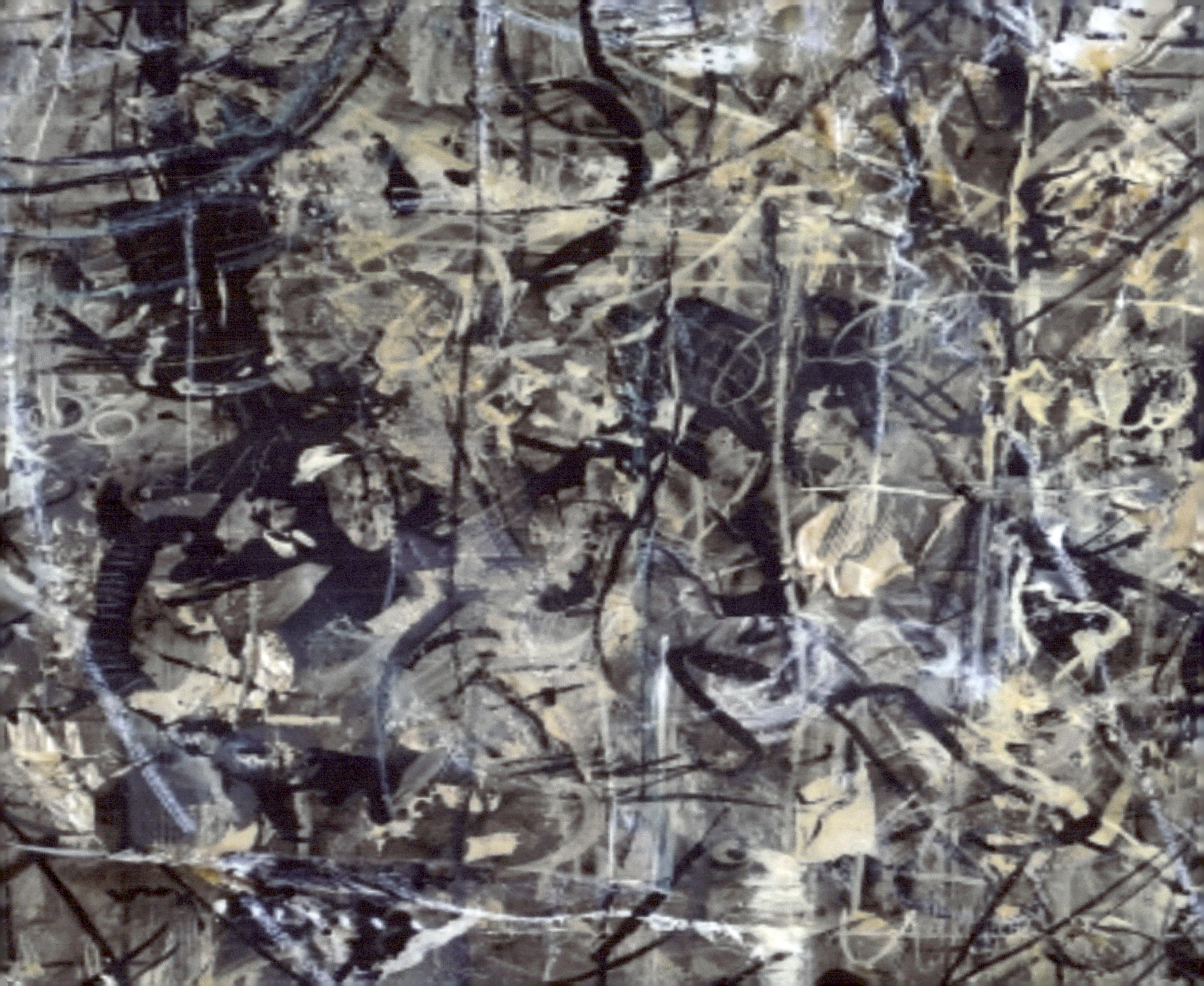